EASY

COPYCAT RECIPES

MAKE MOST POPULAR DISHES AT HOME.
DELICIOUS RECIPES, FROM APPETIZERS TO
DESSERTS, BY OLIVE GARDEN, PF CHANG'S
AND MORE.

Angela Cook

TABLE OF CONTENT

INTRODUCTION 7

APPETIZERS AND SIDES 9

    GREEN BEAN CRISPERS...11
    BEER CHEESE 13
    ORIENTAL CHICKEN SALAD 15
    BUSHMAN MUSHROOMS...17

SNACKS..19

    PF CHANG'S LETTUCE WRAPS..21
    POTATO BOATS 23
    BUSHMAN BREAD 25
    OUTBACK'S HONEY WHOLE WHEAT BREAD 27

SOUPS 29

    P.F. CHANG'S CHEF JOHN'S CHICKEN LETTUCE WRAPS...............................31
    DISNEYLAND'S MONTEREY CLAM CHOWDER 33
    APPLE WALNUT CHICKEN SALAD 35
    CHEESY WALKABOUT SOUP...38

CHICKEN 41

    CHICKEN QUESADILLA 43
    PEI WEI'S SESAME CHICKEN 45
    PEI WEI'S COCONUT CURRY WITH CHICKEN 48
    ALICE SPRINGS CHICKEN 50

BEEF AND PORK...53

    PF CHANG'S PEPPER STEAK..55
    OUTBACK STYLE STEAK..57
    TERIYAKI FILET MEDALLIONS...59

SEAFOOD...61

    SHRIMP BROCCOLI CAVATAPPI 64
    PF CHANG'S KUNG PAO SHRIMP 67
    PF CHANG'S SHRIMP DUMPLINGS 69

VEGETARIAN RECIPES..71

    VEGGIE PATCH PIZZA 73
    VEGETABLE MEDLEY 75
    PF CHANG'S SHANGHAI CUCUMBERS 77

PASTA **79**

    OLIVE GARDEN'S FETTUCCINE ALFREDO 81
    RED LOBSTER'S SHRIMP PASTA 83
    CHEESECAKE FACTORY'S CAJUN JAMBALAYA PASTA 85
    CALIFORNIA PIZZA KITCHEN'S KUNG PAO SPAGHETTI 88
    CYCLONE CHICKEN PASTA 91

DESSERT **93**

    MAPLE BUTTER BLONDIE 95
    APPLE CHIMI CHEESECAKE 97
    P.F. CHANG'S COCONUT PINEAPPLE ICE CREAM WITH BANANA SPRING ROLLS 99
    PUMPKIN CHEESECAKE 102

DRINKS **105**

    STARBUCKS GRAHAM LATTE 107
    STARBUCKS BIRTHDAY FRAPPUCCINO 109
    STARBUCKS PUMPKIN SPICE LATTE 110
    SALTED CARAMEL FRAPPUCCINO 112

CONCLUSION **115**

APPENDIX - COOKING CONVERSION CHARTS **117**

Introduction

Meals at the restaurant are the greatest. We always eat in our favorite restaurants, but it's sometimes hard to drink the motivation to leave home comforts and invest $15 on dinner. This is why we are pleased that a number of meals from our favorite chains (guilty fast food, and so on) were recreated there by food bloggers and other great chefs. You may thank these geniuses for enabling you to whip up anything you want and eat while you were lazy on your own couch.

Whether you are fascinated with the food, or unconsciously addicted to P.F. Chang's Mongolian Pork, presumably for it there's a copycat version. What enhances it is that they sometimes even have a way to make the food better — and you can know it is created from fresh ingredients.

The pleasures of sharing a home-cooked meal

Cooking helps together families and home cooking is a great way for your family to get together over the dining table. Everyone enjoys a home-cooked meal— particularly moody teens and chicken eaters. And if you stay home, that's not preparing or dining either. Sharing meals with others is a great way to broaden the social network. Getting thankful feedback on a meal that you prepared for someone may also give your self-esteem a real boost.

Consider your meals a shared activity. The simple act of talking to a friend or a lover at the table will play an important role in alleviating tension and improving mood. Gather the kids together and keep up with each other's everyday life. Invite a relative, partner or neighbor if you stay alone.

Turn the displays off. Please stop at the Television, turn off your cell and remove any disruptions, so you can really listen to the person with whom you share a meal. You can also prevent overcrowding by minimizing phones and dining with others.

Eat with others. Fish with others. Invite your spouse, coworker or friend to share the responsibility for shopping and cooking—for example, you prepare your entry, the other dessert. Cooking with others can be a fun way to improve your partnerships and sharing expenses can make both of you healthier.

Copycat recipes will let you get the taste of these dishes in the comfort of your own home. For the ingredients, you will find most of what is needed in the Asian food aisle of your supermarket or grocery store, for wontons or egg roll wrappers in the freezer Chinese food section, and in the fresh produces for vegetables and fruits. If you have an Asian or Chinese or any other market in your area, that's even better as you will have more options for brands. For stir-fries, I recommend the use of a wok, but a deep skillet will do just fine.

If you want a finger-licking delicious meal from your most favorite restaurant, but somehow you just can't visit the place, then do try them yourself right in the comfort of your home! You can serve the restaurant's special on all occasions and festive meals. You name a recipe from your favorite steakhouse, and we probably have it for you. We present you the best appetizers, refreshing salads, appealing sandwiches or burgers, juicy steaks/grills, and delicious dessert recipes from all your favorite American steakhouses. The good thing is that, while making those recipes at home, you get to control the level of spices; you can reduce the salt and even add some extra vegetables for the kids. You will also save money. These top-rated recipes are proven and perfect specialties for your next restaurant-inspired dinner at home. Your homemade dish should taste like a famous restaurant. You want to impress your guests and be the exceptional host or hostess you always hope to be. Now you surely can.

Appetizers and Sides

Green Bean Crispers

These crispy little treats make you think you are eating something bad for you, but hey, they are vegetables, right? One of the most popular recipes at Applebee's can now be made at home.

Preparation Time: 10 minutes
Cooking time 15 minutes
Servings 4

Ingredients	Directions
• For the green beans: • 1-pound fresh green beans, washed, ends trimmed • 1 cup all-purpose flour • 1 ½ cups beer • 1–2 cups light oil, for frying • Salt and pepper to taste	1. For the green bean crisps 2. Place the oil in a large sauté pan and heat over medium-high heat. 3. In a large bowl, mix the flour and beer until there are no lumps. 4. Work in small batches. Begin by coating the green beans in the batter mix.

- For the lemon garlic aioli:
- ½ cup mayonnaise
- ½ lemon, zest and juice
- 1 teaspoon mustard powder
- ½ teaspoon garlic powder
- Salt and pepper to taste

Shake off any excess batter and fry for 2–4 minutes.
5. Place on paper towel to allow oil to drain and cool. Season with salt and pepper to taste. Repeat for the next batch of green beans.
6. For the lemon garlic aioli
7. Combine all the ingredients until creamy. Keep refrigerated.

Nutritions

Calories: 920 Total Fat: 69g Carbs: 66g Protein: 8g Fiber: 7g

Beer Cheese

This cheese dip on Applebee's appetizer menu is the perfect accompaniment for soft pretzels, hard pretzels, or your finger. It's that good! This recipe allows you to make a similar version at home.

Preparation Time: 10 minutes
Cooking time 2 minutes
Servings 2–4

Ingredients	Directions
3 tablespoons butter	Melt the butter in a saucepan
3 tablespoons flour	over medium heat.
½ cup milk	
1 bottle beer	
3 cloves garlic, minced	
1 tablespoon prepared mustard	

1 teaspoon Worcestershire sauce
1 ½ cups pepper jack cheese, shredded
1 ½ cups sharp cheddar cheese, shredded
1 teaspoon hot sauce, or to taste
Paprika or cayenne pepper, to garnish

Whisk in the flour and continue to stir until the flour starts to brown. Next, gradually whisk in the milk and cook for a few minutes until it begins to thicken. Stir in the beer. Add the garlic, mustard, and Worcestershire sauce, and stir constantly until thickened. Remove the saucepan from the heat and stir in the cheese and hot sauce. Garnish with paprika or cayenne.

Nutritions

Calories: 80 Total Fat: 6g Carbs: 3g Protein: 4g Fiber: 0g

Oriental Chicken Salad

Another menu favorite, Applebee's Oriental Chicken Salad is a must try. This recipe is close to the original and will satisfy you between visits to the restaurant.

Preparation Time: 15 minutes
Cooking time 20 minutes
Servings 4

Ingredients	Directions
For the chicken: • 1 ½ pounds chicken tenders • ¼ cup buttermilk • ¼ cup soy sauce	1. Combine the chicken tenders with all the other chicken ingredients EXCEPT the breadcrumbs. Marinate at room

- 1 tablespoon rice vinegar
- 1 tablespoon sesame oil
- 2 cloves garlic, crushed and minced
- 1 teaspoon fresh ginger, grated
- 1 teaspoon sriracha sauce
- 2 cups panko breadcrumbs

For the salad:
- 5 cups chopped romaine lettuce (about 1 head)
- 1 ½ cups shredded red cabbage
- 1 ½ cups shredded carrots
- ⅓ cup toasted sliced almonds
- ⅓ cup chow mein noodles
- 2 green onions, chopped

For the dressing:
- 3 tablespoons honey
- 1 ½ tablespoons rice wine vinegar
- ¼ cup mayonnaise
- 1 teaspoon Dijon mustard
- ¼ teaspoon sesame oil
- Pinch red pepper flakes
- Salt and pepper, to taste

temperature for 30 minutes.
2. Preheat the oven to 350°F. Coat a baking sheet with foil and spray the foil with cooking spray.
3. Remove the chicken pieces from the bag and dip them into the panko crumbs, pressing to coat. Arrange the chicken on the sheet and bake for 20 minutes.
4. Remove the chicken from the oven and let it cool, then slice it on the diagonal into bite-sized pieces.
5. In a small bowl, whisk together everything for the dressing.
6. In a large bowl, combine the romaine lettuce, red cabbage, and carrots. Divide the mixture onto serving plates.
7. Top with chicken pieces, and drizzle with dressing, followed by almonds, chow mein noodles, and green onions.

Nutritions

Calories: 254 Total Fat: 18g Carbs: 3.3g Protein: 19g Fiber: 0.4g

Bushman Mushrooms

The famous Bushman mushrooms will leave you breathless!

Preparation Time: 30 minutes
Cooking time 30 minutes
Servings 8–10

Ingredients	Directions
Spicy Horseradish Dipping Sauce: • 2 cloves garlic, minced • ½ cup mayonnaise • 1 tablespoon horseradish • 2 teaspoons ketchup • ½ teaspoon paprika • ½ teaspoon salt	1. Combine the ingredients for the dipping sauce and mix well. Cover and keep it cold in the fridge. 2. Prepare the batter by combining the dry ingredients and then whisking in the buttermilk

- ¼ teaspoon black pepper
- ¼ teaspoon dried oregano
- ¼ teaspoon cayenne pepper

For the mushrooms:
- ½ cup chickpea flour
- 1 teaspoon salt
- ½ teaspoon black pepper
- ½ teaspoon mustard powder
- ¼ teaspoon paprika
- ½ cup buttermilk
- 1 tablespoon olive oil
- 1 pound mushrooms, stems on but trimmed
- Oil sufficient for frying

and oil. The batter will be thick.

3. Use a dry paper towel or brush to clean the mushrooms, do not get them wet.

4. Heat the oil to 375°F and fry the mushrooms in batches for 5 minutes. Remove them from the oil for 10 minutes.

5. While the mushrooms rest, heat the oil to 425°F. Fry them again, this time for 10 minutes or until golden.

6. Drain the mushrooms on paper towels and serve them hot with a side of the horseradish sauce.

Nutritions

Calories: 680 Total Fat: 60g Carbs: 28g Protein: 8g Fiber: 5g

Snacks

PF Chang's Lettuce Wraps

This is probably one of the most beloved appetizers on PF Chang's menu. This copycat recipe lets you make them at home any time you get the craving.

Preparation Time: 10 minutes
Cooking time 10 minutes
Servings 4

Ingredients	Directions
• 1 tablespoon olive oil • 1-pound ground chicken • 2 cloves garlic, minced • 1 onion, diced • ¼ cup hoisin sauce • 2 tablespoons soy sauce	1. Add the oil to a deep skillet or saucepan and heat over medium-high heat. When hot, add the chicken and cook until it is completely cooked through. Stir while

- 1 tablespoon rice wine vinegar
- 1 tablespoon ginger, freshly grated
- 1 tablespoon Sriracha (optional)
- 1 (8-ounce) can whole water chestnuts, drained and diced
- 2 green onions, thinly sliced
- Kosher salt and freshly ground black pepper to taste
- 1 head iceberg lettuce

cooking to make sure it is properly crumbled.

2. Drain any excess fat from the skillet, then add the garlic, onion, hoisin sauce, soy sauce, ginger, sriracha and vinegar. Cook until the onions have softened, then stir in the water chestnuts and green onion and cook for another minute or so. Add salt and pepper to taste.

3. Serve with lettuce leaves and eat by wrapping them up like a taco.

Nutritions

Calories: 730 Total Fat: 240g Carbs: 81g Protein: 38g Fiber: 8g

Potato Boats

Everyone loves potato skins! Here's how they make them at Outback – it's so easy you can make them for any occasion.

Preparation Time: 10 minutes
Cooking time 40 minutes
Servings 4

Ingredients	Directions
<ul><li>4 russet potatoes, scrubbed</li><li>¼ cup olive oil</li><li>½ cup shredded cheddar cheese</li><li>6 strips bacon, cooked and crumbled</li></ul>	1. Preheat the oven to 450°F and coat a small baking sheet cooking spray. 2. Microwave the potatoes for 10–15 minutes, until they are tender inside.

- 2 green onions, chopped
- Sour cream for serving

3. Halve the potatoes on a cutting board and scoop out the flesh, leaving a quarter of an inch of potato in the skin.
4. Brush the potatoes inside and out with olive oil. Arrange them on the baking sheet and bake for 10 minutes.
5. Turn the potatoes over and bake them on the other side for 10 minutes.
6. Turn the oven to broil. Divide the cheese among the potato boats and broil for 3–5 minutes, until melted and beginning to brown.
7. Sprinkle with bacon and green onion and serve with sour cream.

Nutritions

Calories: 340 Total Fat: 24g Carbs: 20g Protein: 11g Fiber: 5g

Bushman Bread

This bread is the perfect balance between light and hearty, sweet and savory. It's easy to make and goes well with just about any meal.

Preparation Time: 1 ¾ hours
Cooking time 30 minutes
Servings 8–10

Ingredients	Directions
<ul><li>1 ½ cups warm water (about 115°F), divided</li><li>1 ½ tablespoons sugar</li><li>1 ½ tablespoons dry yeast</li><li>½ cup dark molasses</li><li>1 tablespoon salt</li><li>2 tablespoons butter, melted</li><li>2 cups rye flour</li><li>3 cups bread flour</li></ul>	1. Warm the bowl of a stand mixer under hot water and pat it dry. Pour in ½ cup of the warm water and mix in the sugar. Sprinkle the yeast on top. 2. While the yeast is blooming, combine the remaining water with the molasses and mix well. When the yeast is frothy,

stir in the molasses mixture.

3. Add the salt, butter, rye flour, and 2 cups of the bread flour.

4. Turn the mixer on low until the ingredients are combined, scrape down the sides, and then let it go for 5 minutes. It should be tacky but not too sticky. Add more bread flour if necessary.

5. Transfer the dough to a greased bowl and cover it with a clean towel. Let it rise for about an hour, until it doubles in size.

6. Preheat the oven to 375°F and lightly oil two loaf pans.

7. Flour a clean work surface and turn out the dough. Knead to remove any air bubbles and shape two loaves, turning any seams under the bottom. Transfer the loaves to the prepared pans and let them rise for half an hour.

8. Bake for 30 minutes, covering the tops if they become too browned. Let the bread cool before slicing.

Nutritions

Calories: 371.8 Total Fat: 5.1g Carbs: 76.1g Protein: 9.7g Fiber: 6.7g

Outback's Honey Whole Wheat Bread

This bread is an all-time favorite, no doubt because of the rich flavors of honey and cocoa. This recipe makes 12 mini loaves, to emulate the restaurant. Don't forget to serve it with whipped butter!

Preparation Time: 1 hour 15 minutes
Cooking time 15 minutes
Servings 12

Ingredients	Directions
<ul><li>1 ½ cups warm water (about 110°F)</li><li>2 tablespoons dry yeast</li><li>1 tablespoon plus ¼ cup honey</li><li>¼ cup brown sugar</li><li>2 tablespoons molasses</li><li>1 egg, lightly beaten</li></ul>	1. Warm the bowl of a stand mixer under hot water and pat it dry. Pour in the warm water, yeast, and 1 tablespoon of honey. Let it sit until the yeast becomes frothy. 2. Add the rest of the honey, the brown sugar,

- 1 ½ cups whole wheat flour
- 2 ½ cups bread flour
- 3 tablespoons cocoa
- 1 teaspoon salt

molasses, and egg. Mix to combine.

3. Add the flours, cocoa, and salt. Knead for ten minutes.
4. Divide the dough into 2 equal parts. Separate each of those into 6 pieces and form them into long rolls.
5. Arrange the rolls on a greased baking sheet and place them in a warm place to rise for 45 minutes or an hour.
6. Preheat the oven to 375°F and bake the rolls for 15 minutes.

Nutritions

Calories: 100.6 Total Fat: 1.4g Carbs: 19.2g Protein: 3.6g Fiber: 2.1g

Soups

P.F. Chang's Chef John's Chicken Lettuce Wraps

If you are in the mood for a healthier snack, here's P.F. Chang's chicken lettuce wraps. It's filling and tasty!

Preparation Time: 35 minutes
Cooking Time: 15 minutes
Servings: 8

Ingredients	Directions
Chicken Mix: • 1½ pounds skinless, boneless chicken thighs, coarsely chopped • 1 can (8 ounces) water chestnuts, drained, minced	1. Mix all the chicken mix ingredients (except the oil) together in a bowl. Cover the bowl with plastic wrap and place in the refrigerator.

- 1 cup shiitake mushroom caps, diced
- ½ cup yellow onion, minced
- ⅓ cup green onion, chopped
- 1 tablespoon soy sauce
- 1 tablespoon ginger, freshly grated
- 2 teaspoons brown sugar
- 2 tablespoons vegetable oil

Glaze:
- ¼ cup chicken stock
- ¼ cup rice wine vinegar
- 4 cloves garlic, minced
- 1 tablespoon ketchup
- 1 tablespoon soy sauce
- 2 teaspoons sesame oil
- 2 teaspoons brown sugar
- ½ teaspoon red pepper flakes
- ½ teaspoon dry mustard

Herbs and Wrap:
- 1½ tablespoons fresh cilantro, chopped
- 1½ tablespoons fresh basil, chopped
- 1½ tablespoons green onion, chopped
- 16 leaves iceberg lettuce, or as needed

2. Whisk all the glaze ingredients together until everything is mixed thoroughly.
3. When the glaze is ready, cook the chicken mix ingredients in the oil over high heat.
4. After 2 minutes, when the chicken is cooked, pour half of the glaze over the chicken mix. Continue cooking the entire mixture until the glaze caramelizes. This should take 10 to 15 minutes.
5. Reduce the heat to medium to low, then add the remaining glaze to the mixture. Cook for around 3 more minutes, constantly stirring.
6. Stir in the chopped herbs (i.e. cilantro, basil, and onion) and continue cooking until they are incorporated into the chicken mixture.
7. Transfer the chicken to a plate and serve with lettuce.

Nutritions

Calories 212 Total Fat 10.7 g Carbs 10.8 g Protein 17.6 g Sodium 332 mg

Disneyland's Monterey Clam Chowder

Prepare a magical dish from the most magical place on earth. This clam chowder soup will definitely take your taste buds on the ride of their lives.

Preparation Time: 15 minutes
Cooking Time: 1 hour
Servings: 4

Ingredients	Directions
<ul><li>5 tablespoons butter</li><li>5 tablespoons flour</li><li>2 tablespoons vegetable oil</li><li>1½ cups potatoes (peeled, diced)</li></ul>	1. Make a roux by mixing melted butter and flour over medium heat for 10 minutes. Flour burns quickly, so make sure to

- ½ cup onion, diced
- ½ cup red pepper
- ½ cup green pepper
- ½ cup celery
- 2¼ cups clam juice
- 1½ cups heavy cream
- 1 cup clams, chopped
- 1 tablespoon fresh thyme or ½ tablespoon dried thyme
- ¼–½ teaspoon salt
- 1 pinch white pepper
- ⅓–½ teaspoon Tabasco sauce
- 4 individual sourdough round breads made into bowls
- Chives for garnish (optional)

watch the mixture closely. Set the roux aside.

2. Sauté the potatoes, onions, peppers, and celery in the oil for 10 minutes using a soup pot.
3. Whisk the rest of the ingredients, including the roux, into the soup pot and bring the entire mixture to a boil.
4. After the mixture has boiled, reduce the heat and let it simmer for another 5 minutes.
5. Season the soup as you like with salt and pepper. To serve, ladle the soup evenly into the prepared bread bowls and sprinkle with fresh chives, if desired.

Nutritions

Calories 472.3 Total Fat 36.9 g Carbs 27.4 g Protein 9.3 g Sodium 771.5 mg

Apple Walnut Chicken Salad

Another delicious salad inspired by Applebee's menu creation. Enjoy it now at home.

Preparation Time: 10 minutes plus
3 hours brining time
Cooking time 8 minutes
Servings 2–4

Ingredients	Directions
For the chicken: • 3 cups water • 1 tablespoon salt • ½ teaspoon garlic powder • ¼ teaspoon hickory-flavored liquid smoke	For the chicken brine: 1. Mix together the water, salt, garlic powder, and liquid smoke in a medium-sized bowl.

- 1 boneless chicken breast, pounded to ½-inch thickness
- ½ teaspoon ground black pepper
- 1 tablespoon oil

For the balsamic vinaigrette:
- ¼ cup red wine vinegar
- 3 tablespoons granulated sugar
- 3 tablespoons honey
- 1 tablespoon Dijon mustard
- ½ teaspoon salt
- 1 teaspoon minced garlic
- 1 teaspoon lemon juice
- ½ teaspoon Italian seasoning
- ¼ teaspoon dried tarragon
- Pinch ground black pepper
- 1 cup extra-virgin olive oil
- For the candied walnuts
- 1 teaspoon peanut oil
- 1 teaspoon honey
- 2 tablespoons granulated sugar
- ¼ teaspoon vanilla extract
- ⅛ teaspoon salt
- Pinch cayenne pepper
- ¾ cup chopped walnuts

For the salad:
- 4 cups romaine lettuce, chopped
- 4 cups red leaf lettuce, chopped
- 1 apple, diced
- ½ small red onion, sliced

2. Add the chicken, cover, and refrigerate for at least three hours.

For the balsamic vinaigrette:
1. Whisk together all ingredients listed EXCEPT the oil.
2. Gradually pour in the oil while whisking. Refrigerate until ready to serve.

For the candied walnuts:
1. In a skillet, mix together the peanut oil, honey, sugar, vanilla, salt, and cayenne pepper, and cook over medium heat.
2. When the mixture starts to boil, add the walnuts and stir until the sugar begins to caramelize. Stir for 1 minute then pour onto a baking sheet covered with wax paper. Allow the nuts to cool.

For the salad:
1. Remove the chicken from the brine and pat it dry with paper towel. Season with black pepper.
2. Place the chicken on a hot grill. Grill for 3 to 4 minutes on each side or until cooked through and juices run clear. Let it cool and slice it into strips.
3. In a salad bowl, combine the romaine lettuce, red

- ½ cup diced celery
- ¼ cup blue cheese, crumbled

leaf lettuce, apple, onion, celery, and blue cheese. Divide it onto plates and pour on some dressing. Top with sliced chicken and candied walnuts.

4. Refrigerate any unused dressing.

Nutritions

Calories: 401.6 Total Fat: 20.6g Carbs: 22.6g Protein: 33.6g Fiber: 5.3g

Cheesy Walkabout Soup

This isn't your average cheese soup; the sweet onion brings it to a whole other level. Serve it for lunch on a cold day, or as a starter to a steak dinner, Outback style!

Preparation Time: 10 minutes
Cooking time 45 minutes
Servings 4

Ingredients	Directions
• 6 tablespoons butter, divided • 2 large sweet onions, thinly sliced • 2 cups low sodium chicken broth	1. In a large pot or Dutch oven, melt half the butter over medium heat. Add the onions. Cook, stirring occasionally, until the

- ¼ teaspoon ground black pepper
- 2 chicken bouillon cubes
- 3 tablespoons flour
- ¼ teaspoon salt
- 1 ½ cups whole milk
- Pinch nutmeg
- ¼ cup Velveeta® cheese, cubed

onions are transparent but not browned.

2. Add the chicken broth, black pepper, and bouillon cubes. Mix well and cook on low to heat through.

3. In a separate saucepan, melt the remaining butter. Add the flour and salt and cook, whisking constantly, until smooth and lightly browned. Gradually whisk in the milk and cook over medium heat until it is very thick. Mix in the nutmeg.

4. Add the white sauce to the onion soup mixture, together with the Velveeta cubes. Stir gently over medium heat until the cheese is melted, and everything is combined.

Nutritions

Calories: 260 Total Fat: 19g Carbs: 13g Protein: 5g Fiber: 1

Chicken

Chicken Quesadilla

Although this is an appetizer on Applebee's menu, it is perfect for lunch or a light supper. This Applebee's inspired recipe is delicious.

Preparation Time: 15 minutes
Cooking time 6 minutes
Servings 1

Ingredients	Directions
• 2 (12 inch) flour tortillas • 1 tablespoon butter, melted • 2 tablespoons chipotle pepper sauce (optional) • 4 ounces grilled chicken (spicy seasoning optional) • ¼ cup pepper jack cheese, shredded • ¼ cup tomato, diced • Optional toppings: • jalapeño pepper, diced • onion, diced • cilantro, minced • bacon, fried and crumbled • 1 cup lettuce, shredded • To serve: • sour cream • green onion • salsa	1. Preheat a large skillet over medium heat. 2. Brush one side of each tortilla with melted butter. Place one tortilla butter side down on your counter or cutting board. 3. Top the tortilla with chipotle sauce, then sprinkle on the grilled chicken. Add the cheese, tomato, and other desired toppings. Top with the other tortilla, butter side up, and transfer it to the skillet. 4. Cook on one side for about 3 minutes (or until the tortilla starts to crisp up), then flip and cook on the other side, making sure the cheese has melted completely, but not so long that the lettuce (if used) is wilted. 5. Serve the quesadilla with sour cream, green onion, and salsa.

Nutritions

Calories: 800 Total Fat: 43.8g Carbs: 52.9g Protein: 44.9g Fiber: 10g

Pei Wei's Sesame Chicken

Sesame Chicken is another Asian restaurant favorite. This recipe inspired by the dish at Pei Wei is sure to please.

Preparation Time: 20 minutes
Cooking time 15 minutes
Servings 4–6

Ingredients	Directions
Sauce: • ½ cup soy sauce • 2½ tablespoons hoisin sauce	1. Prepare the sauce by whisking all of the ingredients together in a small saucepan. Bring to a

- ½ cup sugar
- ¼ cup white vinegar
- 2½ tablespoons rice wine
- 2½ tablespoons chicken broth
- Pinch of white pepper
- 1¼ tablespoons orange zest

Breaded chicken:
- 2 pounds boneless skinless chicken breasts
- ¼ cup cornstarch
- ½ cup flour
- 1 egg
- 2 cups milk
- Pinch of white pepper
- Pinch of salt
- 1-quart vegetable oil
- ½ red bell pepper, chunked
- ½ white onion, chunked
- 1 tablespoon Asian chili sauce
- ½ tablespoon ginger, minced
- ¼ cup scallions, white part only, cut into rings
- 1 tablespoon sesame oil
- 1 tablespoon cornstarch
- 1 tablespoon water
- Sesame seeds for garnish

simmer, then remove from the heat and set aside.

2. Whisk the eggs, milk, salt and pepper together in a shallow dish.
3. Mix the ¼ cup of cornstarch and flour together in a separate shallow dish.
4. Dredge the chicken pieces in the egg mixture and then in the cornstarch/flour mixture. Shake off any excess, then set aside.
5. Heat the vegetable oil over medium-high heat in a deep skillet or saucepan.
6. When hot, drop the coated chicken into the oil and cook for about 2–4 minutes. Remove from oil and place on a paper-towel-lined plate to drain.
7. Make a slurry out of the 1 tablespoon of cornstarch and water.
8. In a different large skillet or wok, heat 1 tablespoon of sesame oil until hot. Add the ginger and chili sauce and heat for about 10 seconds.
9. Add the peppers and onions and cook for another 30 seconds. Stir in the chili sauce and ginger and the sauce you made earlier and bring to a boil. Once it boils, stir in the cornstarch slurry and cook until the sauce thickens.

10. When the sauce is thick, add the chicken and stir to coat.
11. Serve with rice, and sprinkle with sesame seeds.

Nutritions

Calories: 293 Total Fat: 14g Carbs: 27g Protein: 14g Fiber: 0.7g

Pei Wei's Coconut Curry with Chicken

Pei Wei's Coconut Curry is delicious. This recipe is pretty close to the awe-inspiring original.

Preparation Time: 5 minutes
Cooking time 20 minutes
Servings 4–6

Ingredients	Directions
• Meat from one whole chicken, or 6–8 chicken tenderloins, cooked	1. Whisk together the coconut milk and green curry paste in a medium

- 1 cup snow pea pods
- 2 red bell peppers, chopped
- 1 yellow or white onion, chopped
- 3 carrots, chopped
- 5 cloves garlic, minced
- 1-inch piece of ginger, minced
- 2 (14-ounce) cans full-fat coconut milk
- ½ (2.8-ounce) pouch green curry paste
- One bunch Thai basil or regular basil, roughly chopped
- Salt and pepper to taste

saucepan. Bring to a simmer.

2. Add the cooked chicken and all of the vegetables. Continue to simmer until the vegetables are cooked through to your desired softness, about 15–20 minutes.

3. Serve with rice.

Nutritions

Calories: 320 Total Fat: 22g Carbs: 8.5g Protein: 25g Fiber: 1.4g

Alice Springs Chicken

This is one of our favorite ways to eat chicken breast, but because of the amount of bacon and cheese involved, we don't do it every week!

Preparation Time: 15 minutes + Marinating time 30 minutes
Cooking time 40 minutes
Servings 4

Ingredients	Directions
For the marinade: • ½ cup honey • 6 tablespoons mustard • ¼ cup mayonnaise • 1 tablespoon fresh lemon juice • ½ teaspoon black pepper	1. Combine the ingredients for the marinade and mix well. Set aside ⅓ cup in the fridge. 2. Place the chicken breasts in a resealable bag and add the rest of the marinade. Turn to coat, and refrigerate for at least an hour, preferable 2–3

For the chicken:

- 6 slices cooked bacon, chopped
- 8 ounces mushrooms, sliced
- 1 tablespoon oil
- 4 (5-ounce) boneless skinless chicken breasts
- 2 cups shredded Colby Jack cheese
- 3 tablespoons fresh parsley for garnish, optional

hours. From time to time, manipulate the bag to ensure everything is coated.

3. Heat a cast iron skillet over medium-high heat and cook the bacon until it is medium crisp. Remove the bacon to a plate lined with paper towels, leaving the grease in the pan.

4. Add the mushrooms to the hot skillet and cook until golden, about 7 minutes. With a slotted spoon, remove them to a bowl.

5. Remove the chicken from the marinade and discard the marinade.

6. Add the oil to the skillet and when it's hot, add the chicken. Do not move or flip the chicken breasts until they are deeply golden, 5–7 minutes. Turn them over and brown them on the other side.

7. Top the chicken with the mushrooms and bacon, and then sprinkle the cheese on top.

8. Transfer the skillet to the oven and cook for about 20 minutes, or until the chicken is 165°F internally.

9. Serve with the reserved marinade for dipping.

Calories: 759 Total Fat: 47g Carbs: 13g Protein: 74g Fiber: 1g

Beef and Pork

PF Chang's Pepper Steak

This recipe pays homage to PF Chang's pepper steak that is served in the restaurant.

Preparation Time: 15 minutes
Cooking time 3 hours
Servings 4

Ingredients	Directions
• 1½ pounds beef sirloin • Garlic powder to taste • 2½ tablespoons vegetable oil	1. Cut the beef into pieces approximately 1½ inches long and 1 inch wide.

- 1 cube or 1 teaspoon beef bouillon
- ¼ cup hot water
- ½ tablespoon cornstarch
- ⅓ cup onion, roughly chopped
- 1 green bell pepper, roughly chopped
- 1 red bell pepper, roughly chopped
- 2½ tablespoons soy sauce
- 1 teaspoon white sugar
- ½ teaspoon salt
- ½ teaspoon black pepper
- ½ cup water

2. Sprinkle the garlic powder over the beef and give it a quick stir.
3. Dissolve the bouillon in the hot water. Stir unil the bouillon has completely dissolved, then stir in the cornstarch until that is completely mixed in as well.
4. Heat the oil in a large skillet or wok over medium-high heat. When hot, add the beef and vegetables. Cook just long enough to brown the beef, then transfer to a crock pot.
5. Stir the bouillon mixture a bit, then pour it over the beef in the slow cooker.
6. Add the onions, peppers, soy sauce, sugar, salt, and pepper. Add ½ cup water around the sides of the cooker.
7. Place the cover on the slow cooker and cook for about 3 hours on high or 6 hours on low.
8. Serve with rice.

Nutritions

Calories: 571 Total Fat: 30g Carbs: 21g Protein: 51g Fiber: 2.5g

Outback Style Steak

Have you ever tried to recreate the flavor of a restaurant marinade, and just couldn't quite get it? Maybe they used a rub! Try this; it's a great copy of Outback's version.

Preparation Time: 40 minutes
Cooking time 10 minutes
Servings 4

Ingredients	Directions
• 4 (6-ounce) sirloin or ribeye steaks • 2 tablespoons olive oil	1. Take the steaks out of the fridge and let them sit at room temperature for about 20 minutes.

- 2 tablespoons Old Bay Seasoning
- 2 tablespoons brown sugar
- 1 teaspoon garlic powder
- 1 teaspoon salt
- ½ teaspoon black pepper
- ½ teaspoon onion powder
- ½ teaspoon ground cumin

2. Combine all the seasonings and mix well.
3. Rub the steaks with oil and some of the spice mixture, covering all the surfaces. Let the steaks sit for 20–30 minutes.
4. Meanwhile, heat your grill to medium-high.
5. Cook the steaks for about 5 minutes on each side for medium rare (or to an internal temperature of 130°F.) Let them sit for 5 minutes before serving.

Nutritions

Calories: 254 Total Fat: 13g Carbs: 56g Protein: 45g Fiber: 3g

Teriyaki Filet Medallions

If you're in the mood for a beef dish that's savory and salty, crisp and juicy, then try these teriyaki steak bites based on Outback's recipe.

Preparation Time: 15 minutes + Marinating time 4 hours
Cooking time 20 minute
Servings 4

Ingredients	Directions
• 3 (6-ounce) sirloin or ribeye steaks • 1 red bell pepper, cut in 1-inch squares • 1 yellow bell pepper, cut in 1-inch squares	1. In a mixing bowl, combine the marinade ingredients. 2. Cut the steaks in 1-inch cubes and place them in a resealable bag. Reserve a third of the marinade and pour the rest over the

- 1 green pepper, cut in 1-inch squares
- 1 large red onion, outer layers cut in 1-inch squares

Teriyaki marinade:
- 1 cup soy sauce
- ½ cup Apple Cider Vinegar
- ½ cup Sugar
- ½ cup Pineapple Juice
- 2 cloves garlic, minced
- 2 teaspoons fresh ginger, grated
- 1 teaspoon red pepper flakes

meat. Seal and refrigerate for 4 hours or more, manipulating the bag from time to time.
3. Soak your skewers if they're wooden and heat the grill to medium.
4. Thread the skewers by alternating meat and vegetables.
5. Grill for 5–10 minutes on each side, brushing often with the reserved marinade.

Nutritions

Calories: 681 Total Fat: 30g Carbs: 32g Protein: 71g Fiber: 0g

Seafood

Shrimp Broccoli Cavatappi

This is one of Applebee's lighter menu options, but that doesn't mean it isn't loaded with flavor. This recipe lets you make an at-home version that is almost as good as the original.

Preparation Time: 10 minutes
Cooking time 15 minutes
Servings 4-6

Ingredients	Directions
• 1-pound shrimp, peeled and deveined	1. Cook the shrimp, either on a hot grill (which will add

- 2 cups dried cavatappi pasta
- 2 cups broccoli florets
- 1 tablespoon butter
- 2 cloves garlic, minced
- 2 tablespoons flour
- 1 ⅓ cups milk
- 1 ¼ cups Parmesan cheese, freshly grated, divided
- 2 tablespoons cream cheese
- ¼ teaspoon salt
- Freshly ground black pepper to taste

that wonderful smoky flavor) or simply fry them in a skillet. Either way, cook them for about 2–3 minutes on each side, just until they turn pink. Keep warm after they have finished cooking.

2. Cook the pasta in a pot of boiling water until it is tender. Everyone likes their pasta a different way, so cook to your preference.

3. Steam the broccoli.

4. In a large saucepan, melt the butter over medium heat. Add the garlic and cook until fragrant, about 1 minute.

5. Stir in the flour and gradually whisk in the milk. Continue cooking for approximately 5 minutes, or until it thickens. Add 1 cup of the Parmesan cheese and the cream cheese, and season with salt and pepper. Whisk together until the cream cheese is melted and the mixture is smooth.

6. Add in the cooked pasta and broccoli and stir to ensure everything is coated.

7. Serve plated pasta and broccoli with shrimp on

the top. Add extra
Parmesan if you desire.

Nutritions

Calories: 520 Total Fat: 22g Carbs: 49g Protein: 33g Fiber: 7g

PF Chang's Kung Pao Shrimp

This recipe for Kung Pao Shrimp is based on the super flavorful dish offered on PF Chang's menu.

Preparation Time: 10 minutes
Cooking time 10 minutes
Servings 4

Ingredients	Directions
• ¼ cup soy sauce • ½ teaspoon cornstarch • 2 tablespoons water • ¼ teaspoon sesame oil • ½ teaspoon balsamic vinegar • ½ teaspoon sugar	1. In a mixing bowl, whisk together the soy sauce, cornstarch, water, sesame oil, balsamic vinegar, sugar and pepper. Set aside.

- Pepper to taste
- 3 tablespoons hot chili oil
- 3 cloves garlic, minced
- ¼ onion, roughly chopped
- 16 large shrimp, peeled and deveined
- ¼ cup roasted peanuts
- 5 scallions, chopped

2. Add the hot chili oil to a deep skillet or wok and heat over medium-high heat.
3. Add the minced garlic and onion and cook for about 2 minutes. If you want to add other vegetables, like broccoli or peas, you can add them now.
4. Cook until the veggies are soft. Add the shrimp and cook for about 2 minutes, then stir in the sauce you made earlier and cook a bit longer until the sauce thickens. Stir to coat the shrimp, then remove the skillet from the heat and stir in the scallions and peanuts.
5. Serve with rice.

Nutritions

Calories: 760 Total Fat: 52g Carbs: 40g Protein: 39g Fiber: 15g

PF Chang's Shrimp Dumplings

This recipe was inspired by the amazing shrimp dumplings served at PF Chang's.

Preparation Time: 20 minutes
Cooking time 10 minutes
Servings 4–6

Ingredients	Directions
<ul><li>1-pound medium shrimp, peeled, deveined, washed and dried, divided</li><li>2 tablespoons carrot, finely minced</li><li>2 tablespoons green onion, finely minced</li><li>1 teaspoon ginger, freshly minced</li></ul>	1. In a food processor or blender, finely mince ½ pound of the shrimp. 2. Dice the other ½ pound of shrimp. 3. In a mixing bowl, combine both the minced and diced shrimp with the remaining ingredients.

- 2 tablespoons oyster sauce
- ¼ teaspoon sesame oil
- 1 package wonton wrappers

Sauce:
- 1 cup soy sauce
- 2 tablespoons white vinegar
- ½ teaspoon chili paste
- 2 tablespoons granulated sugar
- ½ teaspoon ginger, freshly minced
- Sesame oil to taste
- 1 cup water
- 1 tablespoon cilantro leaves

4. Spoon about 1 teaspoon of the mixture into each wonton wrapper. Wet the edges of the wrapper with your finger, then fold up and seal tightly.
5. Cover and refrigerate for at least an hour.
6. In a medium bowl, combine all of the ingredients for the sauce and stir until well combined.
7. When ready to serve, boil water in a saucepan and cover with a steamer. You may want to lightly oil the steamer to keep the dumplings from sticking. Steam the dumplings for 7–10 minutes.
8. Serve with sauce.

Nutritions
Calories: 60 Total Fat: 2g Carbs: 6g Protein: 4g Fiber: 0g

Vegetarian Recipes

Veggie Patch Pizza

Veggie Patch Pizza is a favorite at Applebee's. As an appetizer, lunch, or a light supper, this super easy pizza is delicious. This recipe is a make-at-home version that is inspired by the original.

Preparation Time: 5 minutes
Cooking time 10 minutes
Servings: Makes 1 10-inch pizza

Ingredients	Directions
• 1 (10-inch) flour tortilla • 1 teaspoon olive oil	1. Preheat the oven to 350°F. If you are using a pizza stone, place it in the oven to get hot.

- ½ cup hot spinach and artichoke dip
- ¼ cup tomatoes, diced
- ½ cup mushrooms, sliced
- Salt and pepper to taste
- ¼ teaspoon garlic powder
- ½ teaspoon Italian seasoning
- ½ cup mozzarella cheese, shredded
- 1 tablespoon Parmesan/Romano cheese, shredded

(Even though you are using a tortilla for the crust, the pizza stone will help make it crispy.)

2. With a pastry brush, brush the tortilla on both sides with olive oil.
3. Place the tortilla on the pizza stone, and top it with the spinach and artichoke dip, diced tomatoes, and mushrooms.
4. Sprinkle the spices on the top of the tomatoes and mushrooms, and top with the cheeses.
5. Bake for approximately 10 minutes or until the cheese is melted and bubbly.

Nutritions

Calories: 151 Total Fat: 9g Carbs: 10.3g Protein: 7.4g Fiber: 1.7g

Vegetable Medley

The vegetables that Applebee's Servings on the side taste so good you wish there were more. This recipe is a tribute to Applebee's side that you can make at home.

Preparation Time: 15 minutes
Cooking time 10 minutes
Servings 4

Ingredients	Directions
• ½ pound cold, fresh zucchini, sliced in half moons • ½ pound cold, fresh yellow squash, sliced in half moons	1. Wash, peel, and cut your vegetables as appropriate. 2. In a saucepan, heat the butter over medium-high heat. Once it is hot, add it the salt, sugar, and garlic.

- ¼ pound cold red pepper, julienned in strips ¼-inch thick
- ¼ pound cold carrots, cut in ¼-inch strips a few inches long
- ¼ pound cold red onions, thinly sliced
- 1 cold, small corn cob, cut crosswise in 1" segments
- 3 tablespoons cold butter or margarine
- 1 teaspoon salt
- 1 teaspoon sugar
- ½ teaspoon granulated garlic
- 1 teaspoon Worcestershire sauce
- 1 teaspoon soy sauce
- 2 teaspoons fresh or dried parsley

3. Add the carrots, squash, and zucchini, and when they start to soften add the rest of the vegetables and cook for a couple of minutes.
4. Add the Worcestershire sauce, soy sauce and parsley. Stir to combine and coat the vegetables.
5. When all the vegetables are cooked to your preference, serve.

Nutritions

Calories: 96 Total Fat: 6.2g Carbs: 9.7g Protein: 2.4g Fiber: 4.2g

PF Chang's Shanghai Cucumbers

This recipe is a flavorful take on PF Chang's Shanghai cucumbers.

Preparation Time: 5 minutes
Cooking time: 2 minutes
Servings 4

Ingredients	Directions
• 2 English cucumbers, peeled and chopped • 3 tablespoons soy sauce • ½ teaspoon sesame oil • 1 teaspoon white vinegar • Sprinkle of toasted sesame seeds	1. Stir together the soy sauce, sesame oil and vinegar in a serving dish. 2. Add the cucumbers and toss to coat. 3. Sprinkle with the sesame seeds.

Nutritions

Calories: 70 Total Fat: 3g Carbs: 7g Protein: 4g Fiber: 2g

Pasta

Olive Garden's Fettuccine Alfredo

Olive Garden's classic Fettuccine Alfredo is a simple yet elegant dish. It's easy to make and delicious to eat.

Preparation Time: 5 minutes
Cooking Time: 25 minutes
Servings: 6

Ingredients	Directions
<ul><li>½ cup butter, melted</li><li>2 tablespoons cream cheese</li><li>1-pint heavy cream</li><li>1 teaspoon garlic powder</li><li>Some salt</li><li>Some black pepper</li></ul>	1. Melt the cream cheese in the melted butter over medium heat until soft. 2. Add the heavy cream and season the mixture with garlic powder, salt, and pepper. 3. Reduce the heat to low and allow the mixture to

- ⅔ cup parmesan cheese, grated
- 1-pound fettuccine, cooked

4. Remove the mixture from heat and add in the parmesan. Stir everything to melt the cheese.
5. Pour the sauce over the pasta and serve.

Nutritions

Calories 767.3 Total Fat 52.9 g Carbs 57.4 g Protein 17.2 g Sodium 367 mg

Red Lobster's Shrimp Pasta

Seafood and pasta are always a beautiful combination. Make this at home and enjoy a special meal.

Preparation Time: 5 minutes
Cooking Time: 30 minutes
Servings: 4

Ingredients	Directions
<ul><li>8 ounces linguini or spaghetti pasta</li><li>⅓ cup extra virgin olive oil</li><li>3 garlic cloves</li><li>1-poun shrimp, peeled, deveined</li></ul>	1. Cook the Pasta according to package directions. 2. Simmer the garlic in hot oil over low heat, until tender. 3. Increase the heat to low to medium and add the

- ⅔ cup clam juice or chicken broth
- ⅓ cup white wine
- 1 cup heavy cream
- ½ cup parmesan cheese, freshly grated
- ¼ teaspoon dried basil, crushed
- ¼ teaspoon dried oregano, crushed
- Fresh parsley and parmesan cheese for garnish

shrimp. When the shrimp is cooked, transfer it to a separate bowl along with the garlic. Keep the remaining oil in the pan.

4. Pour the clam or chicken broth into the pan and bring to a boil.
5. Add the wine and adjust the heat to medium. Keep cooking the mixture for another 3 minutes.
6. While stirring the mixture, reduce the heat to low and add in the cream and cheese. Keep stirring.
7. When the mixture thickens, return the shrimp to the pan and throw in the remaining ingredients (except the pasta).
8. Place the pasta in a bowl and pour the sauce over it.
9. Mix everything together and serve. Garnish with parsley and parmesan cheese, if desired.

Nutritions

Calories 590 Total Fat 26 g Carbs 54 g Protein 34 g Sodium 1500 mg

Cheesecake Factory's Cajun Jambalaya Pasta

If the last seafood pasta wasn't quite what you were looking for, here is another one that you may like even more.

Preparation Time: 10 minutes
Cooking Time: 40 minutes
Servings: 4

Ingredients	Directions
Cajun Seasoning Blend: • 1 teaspoon white pepper • 1 teaspoon cayenne pepper • 3 teaspoons salt • 1 teaspoon paprika	1. Mix all of the Cajun seasoning blend ingredients together to make the seasoning. Divide the seasoning into 3 equal parts.

- ½ teaspoon garlic powder
- ½ teaspoon onion powder

Chicken and Shrimp:
- 2 boneless skinless chicken breasts, halved, cut into bite-size pieces
- ½ pound large shrimp, peeled, deveined
- 1 tablespoon olive oil
- Pasta:
- 5 quarts water
- 6 ounces fettuccine
- 6 ounces spinach fettuccine

Jambalaya:
- 1 tablespoon olive oil
- 2 medium tomatoes, chopped
- 1 medium onion, sliced
- 1 green bell pepper, sliced
- 1 red bell pepper, sliced
- 1 yellow bell pepper, sliced
- 1½ cups chicken stock
- 1 tablespoon cornstarch
- 2 tablespoons white wine
- 2 teaspoons arrowroot powder
- 2 teaspoons fresh parsley, chopped

2. Coat the chicken and shrimp with ⅓ of the seasoning each.
3. Cook pasta according to package directions.
4. While waiting for the pasta, sauté the spiced chicken in heated oil in a large skillet.
5. When the chicken starts turning brown, stir in the shrimp and cook until the chicken is cooked though and shrimp turn pink.
6. Transfer the chicken and shrimp to a plate and set aside.
7. Using the same pan, warm the oil for the jambalaya over medium heat. Add the tomatoes, onions, peppers, and remaining 1/3 of the seasoning mix. Sauté for 10 minutes.
8. When the vegetables turn brownish-black, add the chicken and shrimp back to the mix.
9. Pour in ¾ cup of the chicken stock to deglaze the pan. Gently scrape the pan to remove the burnt particles. Turn the heat to high and allow the mixture to cook.
10. When the broth has evaporated completely, add in the remaining stock and cook for another 5 minutes.

11. Turn the heat down to low and leave the mixture to rest overheat. In a bowl, mix the white wine and arrowroot until it dissolves.
12. Add the mixture to the jambalaya. Turn the heat to low and leave the mixture to simmer.
13. When the jambalaya and pasta are done, assemble the dish by:
14. Putting the pasta as the first layer;
15. Covering the pasta with the jambalaya sauce; and
16. Garnish each plate with parsley.

Nutritions

Calories 563.9 Total Fat 13.3 g Carbs 73.8 g Protein 35.9 g Sodium 1457.6 mg

California Pizza Kitchen's Kung Pao Spaghetti

You may not think of CPK as an Asian restaurant, but their Kung Pao Spaghetti is legendary. This recipe pays tribute to the restaurant's version and allows you to make it at home.

Preparation Time: 10 minutes
Cooking time 10 minutes
Servings 4–6

Ingredients	Directions
• 1 cup chicken stock	1. Make the sauce by whisking together the

- 4 tablespoons cornstarch, divided
- ¾ cup soy sauce
- ½ cup sherry
- 3 tablespoons chili paste with garlic
- ¼ cup sugar
- 2 tablespoons red wine vinegar
- 2 tablespoons sesame oil
- 2 egg whites
- ½ teaspoon salt
- 1-pound spaghetti
- ¼ cup olive oil
- 1-pound boneless skinless chicken breast, cut into ¾-inch cubes
- 10–15 whole Chinese dried red chili peppers; DO NOT eat these, they are for color and heat!
- 1 cup unsalted dry roasted peanuts
- ¼ cup garlic, minced
- 3 cups green onions, greens and white parts, coarsely chopped

chicken stock and 2 tablespoons of cornstarch. Stir until the cornstarch dissolves.

2. Whisk in the soy sauce, sherry, chili paste, sugar, vinegar and sesame oil. Bring to a boil.

3. Turn the heat down and simmer until the sauce thickens, about 20 minutes.

4. In a small mixing bowl, whisk together the egg whites, 2 tablespoons of cornstarch and salt. Stir until well blended, but not so much that the egg whites froth.

5. Bring salted water to a fast boil in a large pot. Add the pasta and cook until not quite al dente. Drain.

6. Heat the olive oil in a large skillet over medium-high heat.

7. Add the cut chicken pieces to the egg white mixture and stir to coat. Carefully add the chicken and egg white mixture to the skillet to form a "pancake".

8. Cook until the egg sets, then flip and cook on the other side. Separate the chicken pieces.

9. When the chicken pieces turn golden brown, stir in

the garlic and scallions and allow to cook for about 30 seconds. Add the sauce that you made earlier and stir to make sure it covers everything. Add the pasta and stir to combine with the sauce.

10. Mix in the peppers and peanuts.
11. Serve with scallions.

Nutritions

Calories: 890 Total Fat: 37g Carbs: 112g Protein: 28g Fiber: 9g

Cyclone Chicken Pasta

This copycat recipe is rich with the flavor of sundried tomatoes, oregano, and cheese.

Preparation Time: 10 minutes
Cooking time 30 minutes
Servings 4–6

Ingredients	Directions
• 1-pound dry penne pasta	1. Cook the pasta according to the package directions.

- 1 (8.5-ounce) jar sun-dried tomatoes, oil packed (reserve the oil)
- 2 large chicken breasts, cubed
- 1 onion, sliced
- 1 cup fresh mushrooms, sliced
- 3 cloves garlic, minced
- 1 cup prosciutto, thinly sliced and julienned
- 1 teaspoon dried oregano
- 1 teaspoon dried thyme
- ½ teaspoon red pepper flakes (or more to taste)
- 1 (16-ounce) jar Classico Sun Dried Tomato Alfredo sauce
- ¼ cup milk
- 2 cups Italian blend shredded cheese, divided

Drain, rinse, and set it aside.

2. Meanwhile, heat a large skillet over medium and add some of the oil from the bottle of sundried tomatoes.

3. Add the chicken and cook until it is lightly browned, about 10 minutes, adding more oil if needed.

4. Add the onion and mushrooms and cook for another few minutes, then stir in the garlic and prosciutto. Season with oregano, thyme, and red pepper flakes.

5. Finely chop and stir in the sundried tomatoes.

6. Add the pasta, pasta sauce, milk, and half the cheese. Mix well and cook to heat through.

7. Serve the pasta with the remaining cheese.

Nutritions

Calories: 302.3 Total Fat: 19.1g Carbs: 19g Protein: 14.3g Fiber: 1g

Dessert

Maple Butter Blondie

Some foodies go to Applebee's just for this famous Maple Butter Blondie. This recipe is inspired by that amazing dessert.

Preparation Time: 15 minutes
Cooking time 35 minutes
Servings 9

Ingredients	Directions
<ul><li>⅓ cup butter, melted</li><li>1 cup brown sugar, packed</li><li>1 large egg, beaten</li><li>1 tablespoon vanilla extract</li><li>½ teaspoon baking powder</li></ul>	1. Preheat the oven to 350°F and coat a 9x9 baking pan with cooking spray. 2. In a mixing bowl, combine the butter, brown sugar, egg, and vanilla, and beat until smooth.

- ⅛ teaspoon baking soda
- ⅛ teaspoon salt
- 1 cup flour
- ⅔ cup white chocolate chips
- ⅓ cup pecans, chopped (or walnuts)
- Maple butter sauce
- ¾ cup maple syrup
- ½ cup butter
- ¾ cup brown sugar
- 8 ounces cream cheese, softened to room temp
- ¼ cup pecans, chopped
- Vanilla ice cream, for serving

3. Sift in the baking powder, baking soda, salt, and flour, and stir until it is well incorporated. Fold in the white chocolate chips.
4. Bake for 20–25 minutes.
5. While those are in the oven, prepare the maple butter sauce by combining the maple syrup and butter in a medium saucepan.
6. Cook over low heat until the butter is melted. Add the brown sugar and cream cheese. Stir constantly until the cream cheese has completely melted, then remove the pot from the heat.
7. Remove the blondies from the oven and cut them into squares.
8. Top with vanilla ice cream, maple butter sauce, and chopped nuts.

Nutritions

Calories: 1000 Total Fat: 54g Carbs: 117g Protein: 13g Fiber: 115g

Apple Chimi Cheesecake

If any of you were fans of this delicious Applebee's dessert and were horribly disappointed to find it is no longer on the menu, worry not because here is a copycat recipe that you can easily make at home.

Preparation Time: 10 minutes
Cooking time 10 minutes
Servings 2

Ingredients	Directions
• 2 (9 inch) flour tortillas • ¼ cup granulated sugar • ½ teaspoon cinnamon • 3 ounces cream cheese, softened • ½ teaspoon vanilla extract • ⅓ cup apple, peeled and finely chopped • Oil for frying • Vanilla ice cream (optional) • Caramel topping (optional)	1. Make sure your tortillas and cream cheese are at room temperature; this will make them both easier to work with. 2. In a small bowl, combine the sugar and cinnamon. 3. In another mixing bowl, combine the cream cheese and vanilla until smooth. Fold in the apple. 4. Divide the apple and cheese mixture in two and place half in the center of each tortilla. Leave at least an inch margin around the outside. 5. Fold the tortilla top to the middle, then the bottom to the middle, and then roll it up from the sides. 6. Heat about half an inch of oil in a skillet over medium heat. 7. Place the filled tortillas into the skillet and fry on each side until they are golden brown. Transfer them to a paper towel lined plate to drain any excess oil, then immediately coat them with the cinnamon and sugar. 8. Serve with a scoop of ice cream.

Nutritions

Calories: 1826 Total Fat: 118g Carbs: 179g Protein: 21g Fiber: 11g

P.F. Chang's Coconut Pineapple Ice Cream with Banana Spring Rolls

The perfect combination of cold, creamy tropical-flavored ice cream with crispy banana-filled spring rolls.

Preparation Time: 5 minutes
Cooking time 30 minutes
Servings 6

Ingredients	Directions
Ice cream: • 1 (13½-ounce) can coconut milk • 1 cup granulated sugar • 1½ cups heavy cream	1. Make the ice cream. Place coconut milk and sugar in a mixing bowl. Mix with electric mixer until sugar is dissolved. Mix in remaining

- 1 teaspoon coconut extract
- 1 (8-ounce) can crushed pineapple, drained
- ⅓ cup shredded coconut

Banana spring rolls:
- 3 ripe bananas, preferably plantains, halved horizontally
- 3 rice paper or wonton wrappers
- 1–3 tablespoons brown sugar
- 1 teaspoon cinnamon
- Oil, for frying
- Caramel sauce, for drizzling (optional)
- Paste for sealing wrappers
- 2 tablespoons water
- 2 teaspoons flour or cornstarch

ingredients until well-blended.

2. Place in ice cream maker to churn and follow manufacturer's instructions until ice cream holds when scooped with a spoon, about 30 minutes. Transfer to a container with lid and freeze for at least 2 hours or until desired firmness is reached.

3. Make the banana spring rolls. Lay wrapper on a flat surface. Position a banana slice near the edge of the wrapper closest to you, at the bottom. Sprinkle with about 1 teaspoon to 1 tablespoon brown sugar, depending how sweet you want it.

4. Sprinkle with a pinch or two of cinnamon. Roll up like a burrito, tucking in the sides. In a small bowl, stir the paste ingredients together.

5. Brush the paste on the edge of the wrapper and seal the roll. Place roll, sealed side down, on a plate and repeat with the remaining bananas.

6. Heat oil, about 1–1½ inches deep, over medium to high heat. Fry the rolls until golden brown, about 1–2 minutes on each side.

Place on paper towels to drain.
7. Serve the rolls with scoops of ice cream and drizzle with caramel sauce, if desired.

Nutritions
Calories: 940 Total Fat: 35g Carbs: 149g Protein: 14g Fiber: 2g

Pumpkin Cheesecake

Preparation Time: 30 minutes + 8 hours refrigeration time
Cooking Time: 1 hour and 45 minutes
Servings: 8-10

Ingredients	Directions
<ul><li>2 ½ cups graham cracker crumbs</li><li>¾ cup unsalted butter, melted</li><li>2 ¾ cups granulated sugar, divided</li><li>1 teaspoon salt, plus a pinch</li><li>4 (8-ounce) blocks cream cheese, at room temperature</li></ul>	1. Preheat the oven to 325°F and grease a 12-inch springform pan. 2. In a mixing bowl, combine the graham cracker crumbs, melted butter, ¼ cup of the sugar, and a pinch of salt. Mix until well combined and press the mixture into the prepared springform pan.

- ¼ cup sour cream
- 1 (15-ounce) can pure pumpkin
- 6 large eggs, room temperature
- 1 tablespoon vanilla extract
- 2 ½ teaspoons ground cinnamon
- 1 teaspoon ginger, ground
- ¼ teaspoon cloves, ground
- 2 cups whipped cream, sweetened
- ⅓ cup toasted pecans, roughly chopped

Bake for about 25 minutes.

3. While the crust is baking, begin making the filling by beating together the cream cheese, sour cream, and pumpkin.

4. Add the rest of the sugar, and slowly incorporate the beaten eggs and vanilla. Add the remaining salt, cinnamon, ginger, and cloves.

5. Fill a large baking pan (big enough to hold your springform pan) with about half an inch of water. Place it in the oven and let the water get hot.

6. Put foil around the edges of your springform pan, then add the filling and place the pan in the oven inside the water bath you made with the baking pan.

7. Bake for 1 hour and 45 minutes, or until the center is set. You can turn the foil over the edges of the cake if it starts to get too brown. Remove the pan from the oven and place it on a cooling rack for at least one hour before removing the sides of the springform pan.

8. After it has cooled, remove sides of the pan and refrigerate the

cheesecake for at least 8 hours or overnight.
9. Serve with whipped cream and toasted pecans.

Nutritions

Calories: 740 Fat: 47g Carbs: 68g Fiber: 1g Sugars: 53g Protein: 11g

Drinks

Starbucks Graham Latte

Preparation Time: 5 minutes
Cooking Time: 10 minutes
Servings: 1

Ingredients	Directions
• 4 oz. milk • 4 oz. coffee • 1/4 teaspoon vanilla • 1/4 teaspoon of Honey • 1/4 teaspoon of Cinnamon • Graham crackers	1. In your coffee cup add your honey, vanilla and cinnamon. 2. Brew a cup of your favorite coffee and pour into your mug.

- Mason jar

3. Mix lightly.
4. Using a mason jar pour in 1/2 cup of milk seal with the lid.
5. Shake the milk vigorously and remove the lid.
6. Place in the microwave for 45 seconds.
7. Slowly pour milk into your coffee.
8. Using a spoon scoop the froth onto your coffee.
9. Place 3-4 Graham crackers in a Ziploc bag and crush them.
10. Sprinkle the crackers on top of your coffee.

Nutritions
Calories: 80kcal Carbs: 7g Protein: 4g Fat: 4g Fiber: 1g Sugars: 7g

Starbucks Birthday Frappuccino

Preparation Time: 5 minutes
Cooking Time: 0 minutes
Servings: 1

Ingredients	Directions
<ul><li>1 cup of milk or coffee (chilled)</li><li>1 cup of ice</li><li>1 tbsp. Vanilla syrup</li><li>2 tbsp. sugar</li><li>2 tbsp. Hazelnut syrup</li><li>2 scoops Vanilla ice cream</li></ul>	1. Add all ingredients to a blender and blend until smooth 2. Top with a raspberry whipped cream.

Nutritions

Calories: 260 Fat: 3.5g

Starbucks Pumpkin Spice Latte

Preparation Time: 10 minutes
Cooking Time: 3 minutes
Servings: 1

Ingredients	Directions
• 1 Tbsp. brown sugar • ½ Tbsp. pumpkin puree • ½ tsp. pumpkin pie spice • 1 tsp. vanilla syrup • 1–2 shots of espresso (or 3–4 oz. dark roast coffee) • 6 oz. hot milk of your choice (skim, 2%, Almond Milk, Soymilk, Coconut Milk – they will all work!) • Whipped Cream (optional) • Cinnamon (optional)	1. Mix brown sugar, pumpkin puree, pumpkin spice and vanilla together until well blended (make sure you whip out any clumps). 2. Add coffee and milk and stir until blended. 3. Top with whipped cream and cinnamon.

Nutritions

Calories: 380 Fat: 14g Carbs: 52g Sugar: 50g

Salted Caramel Frappuccino

Preparation Time: 5 minutes
Cooking Time: 5 minutes
Servings: 1

Ingredients	Directions
<ul><li>1 cup coffee (I like to use Starbucks brand coffee)</li><li>2 tablespoons caramel syrup</li><li>1/4 teaspoon kosher salt</li><li>1 cup milk</li></ul>	1. To make this Starbucks Drink Copycat you are going to get started the night before. 2. Brew your coffee, I like to make a full pot of Starbucks brand coffee because then it is even better, but you really can use any brand of coffee. 3. After you brew your coffee pour it into a plastic pitcher. Then add the caramel and salt and stir. 4. Put your pitcher of coffee in the fridge so it cools overnight. Then pour the milk into ice cube trays and put in the freezer to freeze overnight. 5. When you are ready to make your Salted Caramel Frappuccino Starbucks Drink, get out your blender and add all of the ingredients into it. And blend until smooth but still a little ice chunky like at Starbucks. 6. Pour everything into a glass, or if you are like me and love the coffee tumblers they work well too.

7. Then top with whip cream and drizzle extra caramel on the top.
8. Add your straw, because we all know that a Starbucks Frappuccino must be enjoyed with a straw! Then sit back and enjoy!

Nutritions

Calories: 225kcal Carbs: 31g Protein: 8g Fat: 8g Sugar: 12g

Conclusion

The biggest advantage of making copycat recipes at home is because you can do anything with it. You can improve on it, do your own twist to the recipe and so much more. You can also be sure that it is safe because you are the one who is making it. Not only that, but you can also save a ton of money because we all know eating out is much more expensive than making it yourself. You have little control over the ingredients in the meal when you eat out. You can't, of course, adjust the dish that you order because sauces, etc. are made in advance.

Now, imagine having all the necessary ingredients at home for a second to cook the same dish with copycat restaurant recipes. So, when you're making a copycat restaurant recipe, you can "wow" your family and guests.

You're going to have them thinking you've picked up dinner from a favorite restaurant just by using these recipes and saving costs compared to dining out.

Trying to guess what the ingredients are to your favorite restaurant meal is eliminated when you use copycat recipes. You simply follow the recipe and slowly recreate your favorite meal.

Having regular meals inspired by your favorite restaurants as a family allows for a healthier, more tight-knit family. Research has shown that kids who live in families who dine together at home are more united, happier and perform better in school.

To sum up, the huge savings you'll gain from cooking at home could be used for more productive things like a family holiday or college tuition for your kids.

Going out for a meal at your favorite restaurant is always fun to most. But what if you had access to the top-secret restaurant recipes that so heavily guard those popular restaurants? Would you go home cooking these yourself whenever you wish?

It is not really that difficult to learn how to cooktop secret restaurant recipes. Some think you need a degree in culinary arts or cooking education so you can cook those secret recipes. I hate telling you this, but anyone can collect the ingredients themselves and cook a fancy meal that tastes like the real thing.

But do top secret restaurant recipes really taste the way the chef served them? Perhaps. You can easily cook your favorite recipes with a little practice and patience.

The advantage of making your own top-secret recipes is that you can add to them your own flavors and spices. You'd just want to cook the basic formula and start adding what you think would make the flavor of the recipe better after a while. You may start to figure out that some recipes might need a little more herbs or peppers to make the dish better than the original!

Cooking top secret recipes from restaurants will also make your friends and family wonder where you've learned to cook so well. Imagine cooking a whole meal that looks like it was the restaurant's take-out food. I bet some friends of yours won't even believe you've cooked it!

Appendix - Cooking Conversion Charts

Measuring Equivalent Chart

Type	Imperial	Imperial	Metric
Weight	1 dry ounce		28g
	1 pound	16 dry ounces	0.45 kg
Volume	1 teaspoon		5 ml
	1 dessert spoon	2 teaspoons	10 ml
	1 tablespoon	3 teaspoons	15 ml
	1 Australian tablespoon	4 teaspoons	20 ml
	1 fluid ounce	2 tablespoons	30 ml
	1 cup	16 tablespoons	240 ml
	1 cup	8 fluid ounces	240 ml
	1 pint	2 cups	470 ml
	1 quart	2 pints	0.95 l
	1 gallon	4 quarts	3.8 l
Length	1 inch		2.54 cm

Numbers are rounded to the closest equivalent

Oven Temperature Equivalent Chart

Fahrenheit (°F)	Celsius (°C)	Gas Mark
220	100	
225	110	1/4
250	120	1/2
275	140	1
300	150	2
325	160	3
350	180	4
375	190	5
400	200	6
425	220	7
450	230	8
475	250	9
500	260	

Celsius (°C) = T (°F)-32] * 5/9

** Fahrenheit (°F) = T (°C) * 9/5 + 32

*** Numbers are rounded to the closest equivalent

CPSIA information can be obtained
at www.ICGtesting.com
Printed in the USA
BVHW091417070621
608934BV00002B/372